Restoration 108

Charlotte Crumley-Arrington

Restoration 108© 2022, Written By: Charlotte Crumley-Arrington

Library of Congress Cataloging – in- Publication Data has been applied for.

ISBN: 979-8-9860732-6-2

PRINTED IN THE UNITED STATES OF AMERICA.

Table of Content

Introduction

Welcome to Restoration 108, the second installment of my 108 book series. I created this playbook with the goal of helping you to restore yourself after overcoming life's trials and tribulations. Many of you may be thinking, *But, Charlotte, what makes you qualified to author this book?* That's an excellent question. Even though I am not a licensed therapist nor a pastor, I teach others through my experiences. I also interviewed others who were happy to share firsthand accounts of how they restored their life. I am a person who has been through some things, and like you, I have made some not-so-great decisions in my life that have affected me personally and others around me. However, I accepted that it was my responsibility to work towards restoration for myself. I have experienced the powerful, life-changing, mind-freeing, loving feeling that comes from the process of being restored. Not only did I manage to go through it and come out restored, but it's also the freest I have felt in a very long time. In addition, I was able to restore some relationships affected by my past choices.

After having gone through the restoration process, I am much more compassionate and humble. I am extremely excited to share my testimony of what restoration is and what it looks like. But first, I want you to know the importance of the number 108 and its significance to this series.

The number 108 is an angel number that has many powerful meanings. For me, the number 108 came to me in a dream I had one night after deciding I would use my gift of motivating others to encourage people to do what God has put them here to do. Seeing the number 108 assures you of the presence of angels in your life. It is a sign your hard work is about to pay off and means this is a time for you to restore your purpose in life. Lastly, the number 108 combines angel numbers 1, 0, and 8. One of the attributes of number 1 is liveliness. Live a life of joy; experiment with new things that will excite you. The 0 is about God and spirituality. Grow closer to God; read books that will strengthen you spiritually. Number 8 is a number that gives strength to the attributes you already have. You will reap plenty from that which you have already planted. That is the attribute of number 8. Therefore, be encouraged.

In addition to my testimony, I will introduce the Restoration 108 Conversations, where we dive into restoring life after divorce, incarceration, losing a spouse or loved one, and mending broken relationships with your children. Through these thought-provoking conversations, you will get to read the stories of myself and others who have been on the journey and were able to restore what we've lost. To make the experience even more personal and to provide a coach's touch, I will include probing questions for you to answer, scriptures for you to meditate on, and tips to further help you throughout your journey. It is my hope that this playbook not only educates you but leaves you inspired to embark on your journey to restoration.

Be Gracious to Yourself

"Be alert and of sober mind. Your enemy the devil prowls around like a roaring lion looking for someone to devour."

1 Peter 5:8 (NIV)

Have you ever been in church, coaching, or a therapy session, and the pastor or person you are speaking with reminds you about the power of prayer, healing, and grace? They encourage you to take all things to God, as He is the center of your joy. They inspire you to heal from the things that happened to you and forgive those who hurt you. They speak into your spirit to give yourself a little grace because none of us walking this earth are perfect. That's all good advice. However, for many of us, we were not taught how to implement the ideals of any of this. Even though the concept of overcoming and getting back to a place of full restoration is a journey many seek to complete, they don't know where to begin.

Since everyone's journey and level of commitment to change will vary, I cannot promise that something will click in your mind after reading this book, and you will be instantly healed. My hope is for you to at least learn enough to take much of the pressure off yourself. Understand that you are human—without a manual or instruction guide to life. We are all flowing through these years, blindly learning along the way. We cannot foresee the future; we are not blessed to receive premonitions warning us of pain and heartbreak before it arises. Thus, why do we continue to beat ourselves up because of the end result? This is where your grace comes in, healing ignites, and the gift of prayer becomes your friend. In this chapter, I want to examine and help you with these three tools so you can utilize them when it comes to restoration.

Before diving into those three concepts, let's examine what I mean when I say restoration. Being a certified life coach, a woman of faith, and a person who enjoys motivating others, the concept of restoration spoke to me at church. I'm sure most—if not all—of you have witnessed the pastor open the altar during church service, allowing people to give their testimony. At first, I did not understand the power and teachings that giving your testimony offered. But as I grew older and started experiencing life's bumps, bruises, and pain, I looked forward to hearing the testimonies shared. Others' experiences let me know I was not alone in my struggles or sacrifices. Also, it grew my faith—knowing if God could do it for them, He could do it for me, too.

Hearing their testimonies reassured me that God is a man of second chances. However, to fully emerge into the new, we must be restored from the decision or act that adversely affected us. Since this is more a therapeutic book than a coaching manual, I want to be sure to provide professional content to validate what I am saying. Is that all right, Loves?

According to the Merriam-Webster Dictionary, the word restoration is "an act of restoring or the condition of being restored, such as: (A) bringing back to a former position or condition, (B) restitution, and (C) restoring to an unimpaired or improved condition." In addition, when we look at restoration biblically, it is "an act of repairing, rehabilitation, rebuilding, reconstruction, and redecoration of something to a good condition or operation. Restoration is also an act of returning something or someone to a satisfactory state. Restoration can take place in both the physical realm and spiritual realm."

Both definitions indicate that restoration is simply returning something to its original state or in working condition. Now I know you may be thinking, *Charlotte, you are authoring a book based on how to go back to the way we were prior to the mistake. Aren't we supposed to grow and move forward?* The answer is yes! Restoration is not only about restoring backward but analyzing past mistakes to move forward better. You see, when it comes to restoring anything, sometimes you have to go back to see where the issue lies. Once you know that, you will know the actions to implement and the materials needed to rebirth the beauty and functionality of that which you are attempting to restore. For example, have you ever broken something you cherished? Instead of throwing it away, you created a plan using glue, tape, thread, or string to put the broken item back together so it would be operational again.

Now fancy this—have you ever put something back together so perfectly that it looked better than it did when you bought it? This is the restoration journey on which we will focus—discovering what is broken and creating a plan so we can restore you to a greater you full of God's mercy, grace, and wisdom. Are you ready to be restored to a greater, more powerful you?

Ask yourself this: *What do I need to be restored from?* When you think about it, this is a challenging question because we all have pain deep in our souls that reside there like an unwelcomed guest. This pain may come to us when we are feeling fantastic or resurface when triggered by a certain memory. It could occur when passing by a particular spot or hearing a certain song. These thoughts are like the devil, looking to devour your joy. Sometimes the thoughts of past mistakes are hard to shake.

I remember being younger and my father drinking his E&J Brandy while talking about past mistakes and hurts. We would sit at our patio bar in the den. He would pour himself a drink, make a Shirley Temple for me, and then share stories of his happy memories and past hurts. I also recall him taking me to our local American Legion Post 310 and repeating the same stories of sadness and happiness. Sometimes he would cry, and sometimes he would laugh. All times, he would drill into me the importance of love, self–love, and being my best.

Fast forward forty years later. I now understand the power those tears carried and what those life-changing memories meant to him. When I start feeling that pain in my soul and thinking about my past mistakes, I tell myself not to go down the rabbit hole—having one bad thought and then another, which only leads to more bad thoughts. Get it? The rabbit hole—a situation from which it is difficult to extricate oneself. I even came up with a melody to help get my mind back focused on happy thoughts when I feel myself slipping into the hole's darkness. I sing my song, focus on the present, and continue to be thankful for where I am, what I am doing, and everything I am accomplishing.

Now that we have a full understanding of restoration and our goal, let's go back to the three concepts needed on the restoration journey.

PRAYER

If you are a person of faith, you are fully aligned with the power of prayer. Prayer is how you communicate and build a relationship with whichever god you believe in. What kind of relationship would you have with anyone if you never talked to them and they never talked back to you? Prayer is a give and receive; you call, and God answers.

The key to answered prayers is given in **Mark 11:24 (KJV)**: *"What things soever ye desire, when ye pray, believe that ye receive them, and ye shall have them."* Thus, to be restored in order to move forward, you must seek ye first the kingdom of God to receive the armor needed to undergo the struggle. Prayer also gives us the comfort of hearing God's instructions on how He wants us to move forward once we break free of what is holding us back physically, mentally, or emotionally.

I'll be the first to say restoring anything is not as easy as one might suggest. Let's refer back to the example of putting something together that was broken. Even though you have a plan and the tools, the pieces will not fit perfectly at times. Have you ever tried to fix something, and it frustrated you so bad you had to step away to save "it" from being broken even more? Come on now! Don't leave me out here by myself, Loves! How many of you be trying to fix that thing, and then in the midst of doing so, something else breaks? Lord have mercy! But instead of discarding it, you step away to calm down. I like to refer to that act of stepping away as "prayer time"—time to seek composure, calm, and instruction. You cannot fix anything in the spirit of frustration. You need to get back to the peace so you can focus with a clear mind. How do you get that clear mind? Prayer!

When it comes to restoration, you must focus on the journey and getting it right so you do not repeat the process. Including the power of prayer in your process will help you find calm when the journey becomes too heavy.

HEALING

When it comes to healing, it needs no introduction. This word is used so frequently, especially with pastors and medical professionals, that we all should be familiar with its meaning. However, for those who are not or need a reminder, healing is the process of becoming well again. According to the Bible, "healing occurs through the integrating forces that restore, transform, sustain, and nurture the whole person (body, mind, spirit) at each phase and in every dimension of life, and within relationships of the person to the creation, to other people, and to God." Restore! There's that word again! Healing is the most important concept in the restoration process as it helps you deal with the internal pressure that affects decision-making and behavior.

Do you need healing from a decision you made or that someone else made for you? Did you make a decision you thought would only impact you, but it ended up also affecting those around you? Or did you allow someone else to make that decision for you? For example, someone close to you asked you to do something, and although you knew it was a bad decision, you did it anyway. As a result, it affected your life in a negative way. Now you not only have to forgive yourself for making that bad decision, but you also have to forgive that person in order to achieve true healing.

Healing allows you to face the issues head-on. To help you understand the healing process, here are the five stages according to Betterlyf.com, which says, "Process of emotional healing escalates the process of creating personal change and transformation with the ultimate achievement of inner peace. An individual passes through five stages while going through the healing process. These stages last for different periods of time and do not necessarily occur in sequential order."

- **Stage One: Denial** — A normal human defense against painful emotional experiences that are difficult to accept. Denial slowly gives way to the acceptance of reality. With time, you will look at your loss and accept it with courage and growing optimism about the future.

- **Stage Two: Anger** — Usually follows the grief and denial stage. During this stage, we ask ourselves, "Why me?"

- **Stage Three: Bargaining** — After dealing with anger, an individual may think if they act or talk nicely or "bargain," decisions may be reversed.

- **Stage Four: Depression** — An unexpressed anger turned inward on the self. It applies to passive individuals who believe they cannot do anything to relieve their suffering. Depression appears as one experiences a loss of self-worth. This is the most difficult stage to be in and makes one feel withdrawn and exhausted. Passive anger needs to be converted into active anger by expressing it, which allows us to see things more objectively.

- **Stage Five: Acceptance** — This stage makes one empty of feeling, as if the pain is gone, the struggle is over, and rest is at hand. It is at this stage that faith develops, and growth follows. A new life is within your reach.

Can I share something factual with you? Healing is not a simple 1-2-3 formula that will lead to the automatic restoration of 100% efficiency of an individual. True healing is not linear, meaning you cannot expect to be undergoing depression today and wake up tomorrow healed. Healing can take months, sometimes years, and there is a chance you will backslide along the way. If so, it's okay because healing is a process and a journey you have accepted, which puts you in a position to win. You cannot expect things in your life to be perfect because nothing and no one is. That is why you must give yourself grace as you heal.

GRACE

Give yourself grace. How many of you have seen this phrase or have been told this by someone? Those three words have become a permission slip for accepting that no one is perfect and will make mistakes. How many of you have listened while a person discussed feeling guilty about not being a good parent or spouse? How about the people who blame themselves for their lives being destroyed, their story so tragic it breaks your heart? Have you heard a child speak of themselves in such a toxic manner that they fall into a deep depression?

When life has beaten you up so bad, and you start beating yourself up, this is when you need to seek grace. What is grace? Dianne Bondy, a yoga teacher and author of the book *Yoga for Everyone*, says, "Grace happens to give us some space, acceptance, and room to take a hard swallow or step back...and practice self-compassion." Giving yourself grace is permission to forgive your mistakes, lapses in judgment, and hurtful behavior because no one is perfect. Rebecca Werts, a licensed professional counselor, said, "As I grew up, my obsessive need for perfection grew. I strived for 110% everywhere I went and with everything I did." How many of you have an obsession with being 110% perfect? How many of you only want perfection? I hate to break it to you, but mistakes, failure, and letdowns are a part of life. However, after pondering the stress, pressure, self-negligence, and self-sabotage she caused herself, Rebecca was able to identify the culprit— unrealistic expectations.

Let's break here for a minute. How many of you have unrealistic expectations? What things are you putting on yourself that you know are difficult and that you alone cannot accomplish? Before we move on, ponder on this and give yourself some grace by writing out your unrealistic expectations.

_____

_____

_____

_____

_____

_____

_____

_____

_____

_____

_____

_____

_____

_____

Now that you've given life to your unrealistic expectations, shift your mindset to believe your very best is enough. You do not have to be perfect. Stop thinking you are expected to show up and give award-winning performances in life. It simply has to be your best. My first book, *The Message 108*, is a playbook about following your dreams and manifesting your heart's desires. The playbook is to be used to utilize your gifts and talents and be your absolute best. We all have gifts and talents that God has blessed us with. **James 1:17** tells us that every gift is from God. We all have different talents and God-given gifts, all of which are important and can be used for God's kingdom. You see, everyone does not want to be the best CEO, coach, entrepreneur, singer, or chef ever to exist. They simply want to enjoy doing what they have chosen to do in life. However, if those things are your God-given gifts, I guarantee you will be the best. Everyone has the power to use their gift to become as successful as they want to be. Focus on becoming the best you instead of trying to be something you are not. It is about you living in the version that is ordained for you by God.

Now, don't get me wrong. I am not saying don't strive for better in your current position in life. However, if trying to be better will drain you emotionally, mentally, financially, spiritually, and physically, then be comfortable at your level. Trust that God will take you to where He has promised you. At times, social media therapists and coaches post content or drill into your head through one of their reels that "you gotta be better" and "mediocrity is not okay." This is why being okay with who you are and being clear on your limitations and boundaries are key to your growth when restoring your happiness and joy. One thing I know is that we are all more alike than we are unalike. When you focus on giving yourself the best based on your capacity, you take the pressure off the need for perfection or meeting everyone's expectations of you.

I must admit there was a time when I was just like Rebecca—not giving myself grace or fully embracing the grace given to me. I was more focused on getting it done and being the best rather than on how I could cultivate my uniqueness. Most of my success was birthed out of "expectation" rather than "my capacity." At times, during my sacrifice and struggle, I created health issues for myself because I lived with unrealistic expectations and the stress of the deadlines that came with them. Oh, yes, you know the deadlines we place to apply the pressure further.

As you restore, here are some tips from Rebecca Wertz's website iridescentwomen.com that I want to leave you with that will help give yourself grace and make the restoration a bit easier to stay committed to.

EVALUATE THE EXPECTATIONS

Stress, frustration, and disappointment are sometimes self-imposed due to unrealistic standards and no boundaries. How many of you are harder on yourself than anyone else? I mean, you are your worst critic. You beat yourself up so well that when someone else does it, you are numb. Evaluate your standards, and ask yourself these questions:

- Who created this expectation?
- Is it healthy, or will this create an unbearable weight mentally, emotionally, or physically?
- Does this expectation allow me to enjoy and grow in the process?
- Is this an expectation I would place on someone else?

When we take a moment to evaluate the expectations in our lives, it gives us the opportunity to know how to respond with grace.

ESTABLISH HEALTHY BOUNDARIES

Once you have evaluated your expectations, you must define and establish healthy boundaries. Boundaries are guidelines, limits, or rules we create to identify and foster a safe environment for us and others to navigate and engage within. Establishing boundaries with ourselves, our responsibilities, and those around us is important. If we do not, we will find ourselves burned out and struggling to identify/meet our personal and professional needs. Boundaries communicate that you know yourself and respect yourself enough not to sacrifice who you are and what you need for the sake of approval, acceptance, or achievements.

EMBRACE THE GIFT OF EVOLVING

This restoration journey will make you take a good look at the man/woman in the mirror and accept the mistakes you have made. God is so gracious that He will bring them to your attention, but it will be your job to rectify the hurt. He will not forsake you, though. God will walk with you and encourage you along the way. Although a painful process, it is needed to be clear about what you're praying for and working to be restored in your life. This is your journey, and you will win.

When it comes to evolving, I want to challenge you to evolve in your lane and not based on the pressure of rushing to give false testimony. Do not evolve without patience and nourishment, as the process of waiting, praying, and healing does not yield a return on investment immediately. God's promises are true; you will be restored. But there will certainly be moments that will be painful during this process. These moments will require change and for you to take a moment to pause and embrace the beauty of evolving into who God desires you to be. I promise you, evolving in your true calling is more rewarding and victorious than trying to be someone you are not called to be.

USE MISTAKES AS LEARNING OPPORTUNITIES

Who likes making mistakes? None of us, I'm sure. How many of you feel like mistakes are the devil's doing, especially those mistakes that are sinful? *That was nothing but the devil! I rebuke Satan in the name of Jesus.* Sound familiar? It's what many people say when faced with adversity. I know I do, but I have to play devil's advocate for a minute and say the devil is not that busy. He is not showing up every minute of the day to purposefully make you do wrong. Sometimes, our mistakes are made because of our own judgment, greed, and desire. Your decisions caused your mistake. Have you ever seen someone run a red light because they were in a rush? In that moment, they thought running the red light was a good decision, but that decision resulted in an accident that would cost them dearly, whether in the form of injury, an increase in their insurance rate, or both. From that accident, they now know to leave earlier just in case a red light catches them while driving. That accident was not caused by the devil but as a result of their own decision. Your mistakes will only be teachable moments when you see them as learning opportunities. Own up to your mistakes and learn from them.

However, if you make a mistake, do not be so hard on yourself; forgive yourself, focus on what you can control, and ask for help, guidance, and direction in the areas you do not have control over. Once again, we all make mistakes; no one is perfect. Most times, "the worst" is never really the worst.

Grace is not a privilege or luxury—it is a gift from God that we must embrace for ourselves and give to others, knowing that life is a journey, not a destination. My prayer is that as you navigate through life, you give yourself the space for prayer, healing, and grace. Know that the goal is not perfection; it is progression (growth). You cannot pour from an empty cup, and you cannot give what you do not have. I hope you take a moment to give your best rather than attempting to be "the best."

The
Restoration 108
Conversations

Restore After Divorce

"However, each one of you also must love his wife as he loves himself, and the wife must respect her husband."

Ephesians 5:33 (NIV)

Restoration from divorce is a journey I know far too well. I can remember going through my divorce in an unconventional way. I did not seek proper guidance for strength or healing from the pain. I behaved in a manner that masked my hurt. I moved on and focused on taking care of myself and my children, becoming blind to the pain, guilt, and shame of a failed marriage. I never stopped to show myself grace. Instead, I moved in gratitude because although my marriage was over, my ex-husband and I were still friends and able to maintain a healthy relationship for our children's sake. I felt I had done all I could to save my marriage, and if it was God's will, who was I to stop the process? Who else felt like that?

Can I be honest, though? I never knew how I was supposed to feel since there is no manual on going from being married to being single. I followed my parents' playbook that they used after their divorce, but my ignorance of life as a divorcee led me to a place only God could understand and comfort me. It took me nine years to feel my pain and the pain I believed my children felt, as well as our extended family. I tried running from the pain; I tried running from the healing. After running for nine years, God finally caught me and made me sit my butt down to heal my soul. Up until this point, I had worn the mask of being great and living life so wonderful that I actually believed it.

One morning I woke up, and it hurt so much that I could barely breathe or move. I managed to drive the 45-minute commute to work amidst so much pain. During the morning pleasantries, my coworkers knew something was wrong with me. Although I told them I was fine, tears rolled down my face. My body was so sore that it hurt every time I moved. My manager ended up sending me home early, and once there, I took some aspirin and a nap, thinking I would feel better once I laid down for a few hours. Nope, not happening!

The next morning, I tried to get out of bed. Ouch! My body still was not right. So, I called in sick and decided to go to urgent care, but they sent me home with some medicine that did not work. The following day, I went to my doctor, who diagnosed my problem and prescribed another medication. Although every move I made hurt like hell, I was thankful we had a healing plan for my body. The physical pain continued for two weeks. However, another thing happened when I got home and laid down. It hit me like an archer shooting an arrow. Bullseye! Right in the heart. It was time for the spiritual healing of restoration my soul needed.

I started thinking of all the people who I hurt with my decision to get a divorce. I thought about my children and how they felt. I thought about my family and how they felt. I thought about my in-laws and how they felt. I thought about all of them. All this time, I had only been thinking about myself and what I had to do to heal my children, not thinking I needed healing myself. It was like I dropped a bomb, left the scene, and didn't see the carnage I left behind. I guess you can say I had my day of reckoning because at that moment, when I could not move, unable to even turn my head without crying, I knew I had some work to do. I knew I needed to make amends for the pain I had caused others, regardless of my reasoning.

How many of you, like me, hide your emotions to avoid

having to explain the pain? We would rather suffer in pain than speak to release and find peace. But, on this day, I suffered from physical and spiritual pain. I was exhausted physically, emotionally, and spiritually. I had to get down on my knees and ask God for forgiveness and restoration. As I sought God's help, he made me face my mistakes and the pain I was feeling deep down in my soul. As I lay there seeking answers, God revealed the pain and sadness my decision to divorce caused others. What I was trying to make about me, He made me understand the trauma I had caused others. I asked myself was I even qualified to help my babies, when I was the one who had turned their lives upside down. At that moment, my heart dropped, and my body stiffened as if a bomb had hit me.

This day of reckoning forced me to take accountability for what I did so I could heal myself and those I had let down. I had to make amends with God. I had to make amends with my children. I had to make amends with my family and in-laws. I had to forgive myself and my husband. I had to show myself grace so God could restore me to my authentic, happy self again. He sat me down and forced me to face my pain, trauma, hurt, and loss. I had to grieve my loss so I could realize my faults and take accountability for my share in the death of my marriage.

How many of you have had God sit you down and show you why you were being disciplined? How many of you have had a day of reckoning where God made you focus on feeling somebody else's pain that you caused? Having that kind of understanding helps you see the whole picture rather than just your piece. I can remember watching inspirational speaker, lawyer, spiritual teacher, and author Iyanla Vanzant discuss her life trials of being abandoned by her mother, molested, abused, divorced, and then burying her daughter. "I did the work," Iyanla rejoiced. "Your willingness to look at your darkness is what empowers you to change." Her testimony of restoration touched me as she helped me realize I was not by myself. When I only had the strength to use the bathroom and go back to bed, listening to Iyanla made me realize the "work" I knew I had to do. Understanding the work before me humbled me, even though I did not know where to start.

As I began the process, God started revealing things I had hidden in my heart for years—things I was afraid to face or buried in secrecy. As He revealed those things, I received bricks of compassion that I used to help me rebuild a stronger foundation. I faced my imperfections head-on and lived to deal with me in that moment.

Restoration for me felt like I was rebuilding a new and improved Charlotte Crumley-Arrington. I had to unlearn, undo, and unforce while accepting, acknowledging, and taking accountability for not only my role in our divorce but for my values, behaviors, actions, mindset, and perspective. It was like God had to break me down and reveal the expectations, limitations, walls, and unhealthy boundaries I had placed on others and myself. I had to humble myself and have a conversation with my children about how they felt and were doing. It was humbling because I could not defend my actions to them; I could only explain. I also had to deal with the shame and hurt I had caused them. I had to go through this process with everyone I felt I had hurt or disappointed. During the process, God revealed things I had hidden in my heart, and I dealt with those things once He brought them to my attention. It was like rebuilding a wall that had been torn down brick by brick. As soon as I had one brick placed, God would reveal another brick that needed to be added to the restoration wall. The entire process took a couple of years, but it was the best thing I could have ever done.

I still have moments when I feel the pain of my decision in the pit of my stomach. That's when I tell myself I have dealt with it, and it's in the past. I am blessed that my ex-husband and I stayed friends; we have lots of love for the children we created together and are thankful for the years we shared being married.

Be encouraged. This process took nine years for me to go through blindly and three years of restoration to become the woman you witness today. Now, let me say that even after all the work I did on myself, I still have moments where I relive my past. However, I combat those moments of emotional tug-of-war with reminders of how blessed I am that my ex-husband and I are friends and that our children are now successful adults with their own children. Despite all the pain, we forgave each other and have a great relationship. I still sing my song about not going down the rabbit hole. The past is the past, and the now is much brighter and more blessed.

When restoring life after a divorce or breakup, show as much compassion as you can to yourself. Divorce can be one of the most emotional and mentally draining processes a person can go through in life. To me, divorce is not just about the two people who are married; it's also about the village of those two people and how they are affected. For some people, divorce is often used to purposefully hurt the other person and make them pay. I have seen people try to break someone mentally and financially because they know the law will protect them. Others use the children as pawns, causing humiliation and desperation for the other parent. If this is your situation, I encourage you to remember the love the two of you once shared that made you want to say yes and be gracious to each other. If you are currently in this process, understand the process of getting through a divorce and know that the emotional rebuild you will face will be different for all of us.

Here are a few tips on restoring in a healthy manner:

- **Believe** — Believe you will be restored. You must go to your quiet spot and ask God to forgive you. Ask Him to help you forgive yourself. Scripture tells us that all we have to do is ask God for forgiveness, and He will forgive us. **Mark 11:25 (NIV)** says, *"And when you stand praying, if you hold anything against anyone, forgive them, so that your Father in heaven may forgive you your sins."* This is important because you seek forgiveness from God and get what you give. So, forgive those persons you felt hurt you.

- **Ask** — Ask God to guide you and give you the words to say to the people you hurt. Ask Him to reveal what you must do to atone for your mistakes. He will tell you and guide you. Ask God to help you forgive yourself because, throughout your journey of restoration, you will feel the pain you have been good at suppressing. You are now going to feel it. So, ask God for strength. **Matthew 7:7 (NIV)** says, *"Ask and it will be given to you; seek and you will find; knock and the door will be opened to you."* Everyone who asks receives; the one who seeks finds; and to the one who knocks, the door will be opened.

- **Listen** — Listen for God to tell you what to do and where to go. He will let you know. **Job 33:14-15**

(ESV) says, *"For God speaks in one way, and in two, though man does not perceive it. In a dream, in a vision of the night, when deep sleep falls on men, while they slumber on their beds."* For example, He may say, "Call so and so, and ask them how they are doing," or He may tell you to go to church today. He might also instruct you to give someone a compliment, especially someone you do not like. With that being said, God has a sense of humor. Remember, throughout this process, you will have your joy restored, be able to laugh, and not take yourself so seriously at times.

Restore After Incarceration

"I was naked and you clothed me, I was sick and you visited me, I was in prison and you came to me."

Matthew 25:36 (ESV)

I've always had a heart for persons within our prison system. Even though I have never served major time, one overnight stay was enough for me. A family member of mine, who is very near and dear to my heart, has been in and out of the judicial system since their youth, which caused me to understand the penial system on every level of life. My first job out of college provided me with the privilege of teaching mathematics and science in a detention center for youth in Kansas City, Missouri. I was promoted to outreach coordinator, where I motivated the youth with positivity and the belief of knowing that prison or the crime committed does not define them. One of my favorite things I would tell my students daily was that we all do stupid things and make mistakes, but not all of us get caught. I wanted them to believe in their dreams and not accept that living a life of crime was their only option for survival. I wanted them to believe that they could change for the better. However, because thirty-five percent of my students were following a family legacy of being incarcerated, I sometimes found it a challenge to get through to them and make them believe they could have a better life.

According to the article "Collateral Damage: The Children of Prisoners" on the website PrisonLegalNews.org, 1.5 million kids in the United States are children of prisoners, and the effects on their lives are profound. "Some estimates are that children of people in prison are as much as five times more likely to end up in prison themselves," says Jamie Suarez-Potts, program coordinator of the Criminal Justice Program at the Boston chapter of the American Friends Service Committee (AFSC). "Most children who have parents in prison are already disadvantaged, from poor communities," she explains. "Prison costs money to the family, from the arrest and ensuing trial, and maybe having to hire an attorney. And there are costs assigned to people in prison—telephone, clothing, medical costs. All these have to come from the family. Not to mention travel costs for visits, which can be prohibitive."

Thus, incarceration for some kids is a badge of honor because it makes them seem strong; for others, it's how they get to see and spend time with parents and family members. For them, doing better could imply weakness, which no one wants hanging over their name. So, how do we combat the generational curses of incarceration?

Working in this environment and seeing firsthand the adverse effect it has on our children and families, it is my hope to help someone restore their life from incarceration, regardless if they have already served their time behind bars, are serving time currently, or supporting a family member who is serving time. One thing I have learned from listening to those who have experienced being an inmate is that it's a mental shift many people have to transform into to survive. Think about it; you go from enjoying the freedoms of the world to following rules and regulations while being ordered around by guards. Then there are the inmates, some with untreated mental health issues, who you are surrounded by daily. So, the day you enter jail or prison is the beginning of your restoration or, as some say, rehabilitation. Even though your process of survival is different from your restoration from release, "sitting down" to pay your debt to society and the families who may have been affected by your crime is time that can transform a person. However, as your coach and counselor on this, I am here to reassure you there is life and success after incarceration.

If you are currently serving, allow me the opportunity to explain the process of release. This way, you are aware of what you are about to face and can be more prepared for it when it comes. Knowing this will also give you an opportunity to focus on your mental and emotional health as you prepare for your second chance in society. The article "How to Justice," released in 2021, shares the following steps when being released from federal prison:

- **Release preparation.** The Bureau of Prison will begin to prepare you for release eighteen months before your release date. Much of this focuses on preparing you to find work after you leave prison. The program includes classes on job search, résumé writing, job retention, etc.

- **Transfer to pre-release custody.** In many cases, you will not go straight from prison to your home. The federal system uses a system called pre-release custody. By law, you should be allowed to spend the last part of your sentence in pre-release custody. This could be in a halfway house, community corrections center, or in-home confinement.

- **Supervised release.** In the federal system, "supervised release" takes the place of parole. You will spend some time after your actual release from custody under supervision. The conditions of this depend on many factors, including the crime that sent you to prison and your behavior inside.
- **Full release.** After completing your supervised release, you will finish your sentence in full. You will not have to report to the Bureau of Prison or anyone else.

Even though this is the federal process, I am sure the process for state prison releases is the same or close to it. I have defined this process as the human process of restoration. To me, the human process of restoration offers you the opportunity to learn, rebuild, seek therapy, and undergo the process of prayer, healing, and repentance. When restoring your life after incarceration, a moment of forgiveness is paramount. Especially if the person entered the criminal life because of family matters (father or mother not present), the need to make money (poverty), anger and the inability to redirect it (mental health), or revenge (paying back someone who wronged them). When restoring your life, you must give yourself permission to forgive and be forgiven. Removing the guilt and taking responsibility for the crime committed will help you understand what is needed emotionally and spiritually. Thankfully, I have never served time. However, I had the honor of speaking with my good friend, Ira Smith, an ex-prisoner who served five years in the California State Prison System. When I asked what motivated him to seek restoration upon his release, he expressed the yearning of needing restoration not just for himself but to rebuild his relationships with his five children. Believing in the power of prayer and manifestation, he began his restoration process prior to the start of his release. Using the method of journaling, he wrote out his vision and dreams so he could speak abundance over his life in the "after incarceration." He used the tools taught through reading, conversation, and survival to curtail his fear and anxiety of the unknown.

Any inmate rejoining society faces "what if" moments that can generate all kinds of emotions. Some experience such great anxiety about returning to the outside world that they commit another crime to remain in jail or return shortly after being released. Being institutionalized and then set free is a battle within oneself that requires professional help and guidance, especially if the person was sentenced to more than a few months. If you have never been to jail or prison, imagine the world operating one way when you went in and then coming out to nothing looking familiar. For example, remember the movie

American Gangsta when Denzel Washington's character, Frank Lucas, was sent to prison in 1975 and released in 1991. He went in wearing bell bottoms during the disco era and came out to folks rocking Air Force Ones and listening to hip hop! Can you imagine his process of restoring his life?

Even though my friend, Ira, only served five years, he lost so much time with his children, and the world he knew when he first went in was not the same world that greeted him when he walked out. Thus, the four-step release allowed him to gain experience before full reentry, which for many is helpful. Now that he is free, he is focused on rebuilding his relationship with his children and has admitted it is getting stronger every day.

"I am able to be the father I always wanted to be while healing my childhood wounds in the process," Ira told me. When I asked him what are some of the motivational factors keeping him home, he replied, "I'm tired of living the fast life. Plus, I am not trying to get my three strikes. So, I am not doing anything that will put me in a vulnerable position."

Let me briefly explain the three-strike system for those who do not know. According to the Legal Information Institute, the "three strikes" or three-strikes law is a criminal sentencing structure in which significantly harsher punishments are imposed on repeat offenders. The three-strikes law mandates a life sentence for the third violation of violent felonies. For example, under California's three-strikes law, a defendant convicted of a felony and previously convicted of two or more serious or violent felonies must receive an "indeterminate term of life imprisonment."

With this law in place, Ira has to tread lightly because the system is already prepared to keep him for life if he gets caught again. Now I know you may be curious about Ira's story and how his life of crime started. So, here it is:

During Ira's childhood, he witnessed a lot of drug usage, i.e., needles, crack pipes, etc. Being the son of a young mother and the oldest of two brothers, Ira took on the role of "man of the house" and embraced "hustling" as a means of helping his mother take care of the household. Much of the money he earned from stealing helped put food on the table and clothes on his and his little brothers' backs.

One thing for sure about breaking the law, eventually you will get caught, and as bad luck would have it, this was the case for Ira. His crime landed him in the big house for five years. Now forced to sit down, he did some evaluating and turned his life around. While in prison, he embraced his love of God and learned how to be a son, father, brother, and man. Raised in the streets, he had no role model to guide him and show him the legal ways available to support his family. You see, when one grows up in poverty, they are more inclined to take a "by any means necessary" attitude when it comes to getting money.

While incarcerated, Ira unlearned the ways of the streets and adopted a new mindset to stay on the straight path. Once he made this decision, God showed up and began speaking to Ira. I call this process the Human Process of Restoration because you are being taught how to assimilate back into society slowly but surely, step by step. But one wrong step, and you're right back at the place you wanted to be freed from.

Once you've made it to step 4, a full release, then what? Well, there's the Spiritual Process of Restoration for those who want it. This is where it's just you and God, one on one. At this stage, ask Him for what you want and trust in His guidance. Most importantly, you must believe. If you don't believe, you will not trust that the voice you hear is God's. You don't want to have any doubt. This means you must tune in and focus on hearing what the Holy Spirit is guiding you to do.

You may be saying, *Charlotte, how will I know I'm hearing the Holy Spirit speaking to me?* I'm glad you asked. If the voice tells you to do something to uplift yourself or someone else, that is the voice of God. He will never tell you to do anything that will hurt you or anyone else. NEVER. And if you do as He tells you, I promise you will not be sorry. I like to call these little tests. You hear a voice that tells you to do or say something positive and encouraging to someone. If you're obedient, you will pass the test. If not, it will nag at you all day because you didn't do as the voice instructed. As for me, I like to be obedient so I can receive my blessings. This goes back to the beginning, where I said restoration is a humbling process. Believe me, it's a humbling experience to say something to a perfect stranger just because a voice in your head told you to do it. Many times than not, God is using you to be a blessing to that person.

For example, have you ever gotten dressed up and felt like a million bucks, but nobody complimented you? I know you're probably the type who doesn't need validation from anyone but humor me. I'm willing to bet you will feel some kind of way if no one tells you how magnificent you look, especially if that someone is your partner. Now, imagine getting dressed up and feeling like a million bucks, then having someone tell you how magnificent you look. You walk away feeling like two million bucks! Be that person to give someone a two-million-dollar feeling. That's power! Now back to the story.

Being open to change, Ira began asking God for what his heart desired. As God's love would have it, during his time away at prison, Ira decided he wanted to be a better son, brother, father, and man for himself and his family.

Again, he didn't have a positive male role model during his childhood to teach him how to be these things. So, in his case, he not only needed restoration but a whole new way of life—one he always dreamed of having while in the midst of the chaos he experienced growing up.

The amazing thing is God showed up and showed out once Ira made that decision! Yes! Ira told me that he started by asking God for what he wanted, his heart's desires. His relationship with God grew more when Ira was placed in a unit with "lifers." For those who do not know, a "lifer" is a person serving a life sentence in prison. Most of the men in this unit were older than Ira, thus offering him wisdom and guidance in hopes that Ira would learn from their mistakes. Although they had lost their second chance, they did not count it robbery to sow their knowledge to help him embrace his.

After a couple of years on that unit and maintaining a record of good behavior, Ira applied and was accepted into the fire camp program. Fire camp is a program run by the California Department of Corrections and Rehabilitation (CDCR). The program takes non-violent, minimal-custody inmates and transfers them to training camps throughout the state to be trained as firefighters. Look at God! As soon as Ira invited Him into his life, God shifted Ira from a prison cell to a trade camp that taught him how to be a better person.

Being in this program meant Ira got to live at the camp location instead of being confined to a cell. He was able to eat better food, sleep better, and have some fun. But, most importantly, he learned a trade he could use to secure work upon his release. During the training, Ira got to work around actual firefighters. I happen to personally know a few, and one thing I can say about them is they are highly intelligent men and women with hearts of gold. They are great family men l who care about the community and are willing to put their lives on the line for total strangers. So, with that being said, God placed Ira in an environment to be mentored—to see with his own eyes what honest hard work looked like, what being a family man looked like, and what it felt like to be able to trust someone to have your back in a dangerous situation. While being trained, Ira also learned what it looked like to work together as a team to do something positive for someone else.

So, you see, once Ira asked, God started moving. God works like that, you guys. Once you ask, He starts moving. He's just waiting for you to ask. There's a gospel song called "Break Every Chain" by Tasha Cobbs. Ira's story reminds me of that song because that is literally what was happening to him. Ira said the most important thing is that he had to believe. He believed he would get out of prison. He believed he could repair the broken relationship with the mother of his children and his children. For the first time in his life, he was able to get his own apartment and buy a car. It has not been easy, but Ira knows for a fact that it has been his belief in miracles and manifestation that has brought him this far. He also knows that although his life is not as recklessly exciting as it once was, all of that has been replaced with a peaceful and productive life full of love from his children. To him, that's priceless. Today, Ira is free, employed, and loving his children.

Life after prison does not have to be a life sentence for failure. If you are working toward restoring your life after incarceration, here are four things you can do:

- **Join organizations for people who were reintroduced into society.**

  There are some organizations that can help you cope with life after you have been released. Joining a group would not only help you ease your anxieties but would help you expand your network as well. You may find some ideas on how you can get a job by talking to ex-prisoners who managed to get it through. By mingling with like-minded people, you can get the support needed.

- **Join clubs to socialize and feel accepted.**

  Your first few days or months outside prison will be

a period of adjustment. Meeting new people who share the same interests may help you feel accepted. Not only that, but you also get to enjoy what you love to do while at the same time boosting your self-esteem. Staying around positivity is the best recourse for staying away from trouble.

- **Expand your skill set or study again.**
Learning new skills and getting degrees will help boost your confidence and increase your chances of landing a job. If you feel the job market is too competitive, you can use your skills to start a business. Offer services to people close to you, build a portfolio, and market yourself to others outside your circle. You likely participated in certificate and livelihood programs while in prison. These programs were meant to give ex-prisoners a new life upon release. Use what you learned to earn money.

- **Trust in yourself and have faith.**
Nothing can beat the power of faith. Scripture tells us this in **Hebrews 11:1 (NIV)**: *"Now faith is confidence in what we hope for and assurance about what we do not see."*

- **Believe.**

  Regardless of what your circumstances look like, you have to believe in the beauty of your dreams. **(Matthew 21:22)** If you believe, you will receive whatever you ask for in prayer. Once you believe in what you can do, you will get through life's difficulties despite your past experiences. Theodore Roosevelt said, "Believe you can, and you're halfway there." Hence, trust yourself and get ready to face the world again! Remember that being in prison was just one stage of your life; it is not your entire life. Now that you have been given another chance to prove yourself, do not disappoint your family and friends. Most importantly, do not disappoint yourself.

- **Be humble.**

  Serving time in prison is not something you would be probably proud to shout from the rooftops because people can and will judge you. However, a part of the restoration process is humbling because you will eventually have to disclose that information to others and may face rejection. **Proverbs 11:2 (NIV)** tells us: *"When pride comes, then comes disgrace, but with humility comes wisdom."*

Restore Relationship with Your Children

"If we say that we have no sin, we deceive ourselves, and the truth is not in us."

1 John 1:8 (KJV)

Restoring relationships between parents and their children is a topic that is commonly discussed during my coaching sessions. In my first book, *The Message 108*, I share my thoughts on parenting and how important it is for parents to understand that God did not create parents to be perfect but protectors and guides. Parents often get blamed for everything that goes wrong with their children. Some people feel that raising a child a certain way will prevent and protect their child from witnessing dreadful things or making mistakes that will result in them losing their freedom, or even worse, their life.

How many of you know a great parent who made extreme sacrifices to provide their child with the best life? Those children lived in the best neighborhoods, went to the best schools, and were well dressed. Their parents made sure they attended the best events, dined at five-star restaurants that served the best food, and traveled the world to experience adventures in exotic places. I mean, they were privileged beyond fault but still found themselves getting into trouble. On the contrary, I know parents who only had the basic necessities and love to offer their children. They suffered from domestic abuse, unhealed trauma, mental health issues, or substance addiction. Their kids were forced to endure neglect and instability. However, they grew up to become valedictorians, scholarship recipients to ivy league universities, and went on to become successful professionals. So, with these two scenarios, the fate of how our children will end up is not solely based on parents.

However, I will not discount the feelings and emotions children have to deal with or internalize throughout either situation. Far too often, children endure things based on their parents' decisions, which may leave them bruised and broken. How many times have you heard children cry about being abused, molested, or neglected due to their parents' choices? What about the child who was forced into foster care because their mother did not feel she would be able to offer them the best life if she kept them? Unknowing what that child had to go through, who do you think people will blame when the child strays down the wrong path?

So, even though parents are faced with blame as it relates to the lifestyle and condition a child is raised in, they are also the cause of unknown and unforeseen circumstances their child may encounter. Moreover, you have situations where parents are aware but turn a blind eye out of fear or not understanding the impact a situation may have on the child. In addition, many parents ignore situations and chalk them up as "that's what happened to me, so it's your turn." We call this generational trauma. This term has been used numerous times to explain the patterns that occur from one generation to another. Licensed clinical psychologist and parenting evaluator Melanie English, PhD, tells *Health Magazine*, "It [generational trauma] can be silent, covert, and undefined, surfacing through nuances and inadvertently taught or implied throughout someone's life from an early age onward."

With respect to generational curses, let us look at the Bible as it is my goal to give you multiple perspectives. Just like generational trauma, a generational curse is believed to be passed down from one generation to another due to rebellion against God. Some may say you are likely under a generational curse if your family line is marked by divorce, incest, poverty, anger or other ungodly patterns. The Bible says these curses are tied to choices. **Deuteronomy 30:19** says we can choose life and blessing or death and cursing. As parents, we must be careful with the choices we make as they indirectly and/or directly affect our children. And how the child responds or how it affects them can either create a perfect relationship or cause a breakdown.

Before we move on, let's address generational trauma and/or curses and how they plague your families and the relationships within. On the following lines, write out what generational trauma or curses have affected your family and how you are coping with it.

_____

_____

_____

_____

_____

_____

_____

Charlotte Crumley-Arrington

Now that you have given life to your generational strongholds, let us focus on restoring relationships. This matter is often brought up by my female clients seeking guidance on restoring a relationship based on a mistake that adversely affected their children. This guidance is one that I find easy to assist with for the simple fact I am guilty of having to restore my relationship with my children. I had to accept the fact that I dropped the ball at times when it came to being the best mother I could be. When facing this topic, I quickly remind women that they are human. And even though they may have the best interest of their child in mind, their heart will cause them to respond selfishly to protect their peace or enhance their desire to be right. But when it comes to restoring, I encourage you to first communicate with your child with an open mind and a non-defensive heart. Allow yourself to understand how they feel. The worst thing you can do is jump on the defensive when communicating or dismiss their feelings because you think your actions were warranted. Even though you have every right to react and respond to matters in your life, you should refrain from denying someone the right to feel how they do because of its indirect or direct effect on you.

For example, take my divorce and how it affected my children. For nine years, I strived to get my life together as a divorced woman starting all over, but I never gave my children the chance to express how my decision affected them. Honestly, I didn't want to know because I would've had to deal with it. Remember, it took me nine years of running before God sat me down and prepared my heart for the truth. Even though their father and I remained friends and protected them from our drama, I dismissed the idea of them losing their parents being together as one unit. So, during my healing process, I had to have those hard conversations with them—being fully present and listening as they expressed how our decision to end our marriage affected them.

One thing about children is they are always at a disadvantage when it comes to their upbringing and their parents' decisions of what to present or deny them access to. As parents, we are their first teachers and the ones who are supposed to protect them. However, we are given a title that tells us to forgo the idea of being human and focus on what our children need and want. For some, merging the two is hard because being a human and a parent can create a lot of conflict. Have you ever been in a situation where the human side of you wanted to take a job offer out of state because it is what you prayed for, but the parent in you had to consider your children? You had to think about how the move would affect their schooling, how they would feel about leaving their friends, and the possibility of them not wanting to go. How many of you had to choose between acting as a parent or being human? How did it make you feel?

Secondly, you must forgive yourself and then seek forgiveness. By having those hard conversations with your children where you understand how they feel while being clear about your battles of being both a person and parent, you can forgive and be forgiven. You must also be humble in these moments because they may not yet be open to accepting your forgiveness. Their pain may be too deeply rooted, meaning it will take them some time to let go. Standing by their side while they heal is a great way to show them you realize you messed up but are there now to rebuild your relationship as parent and child.

Consistently "showing up" for your child will help them along in their journey of forgiveness, causing them to slowly lower their guard to let you back in. However, keep in mind that restoring a broken relationship is a process. One conversation is not going to make it all better. Children are human, too. Once you have hurt a child's feelings, harmed them in any way, or lost their trust, it is hard for them just to let it go. For some reason, being hurt by their parent is more painful than if the hurt was done by someone else. That's because they feel you should never betray or let them down since you are their mother or father. For some, the pain of being hurt by their parent is unforgivable. But even though seeking forgiveness is not an effortless process, it is a process that can bring you closer together. Again, no person is perfect, and if God can forgive us daily, we can also forgive each other.

If you are going through restoring your relationship with your child, I want to encourage you to apply grace. I have worked with women who lost their children due to being incarcerated, and their children were placed within the foster care system. Can you imagine giving birth to a child you wanted, but because of a bad decision you made, your child is ripped from your arms for a "system" to raise until you are released from prison or until another family adopts them? This reminds me of Antwone Fisher. His father was killed, and his teenage mother gave birth to him while incarcerated. He was placed in an orphanage, waiting for his mother to claim him upon her release. When she never came, Mr. Fisher was placed in a foster home where he was molested and suffered years of physical and emotional abuse. The one thing that got me about his story was when he finally found his mother, he asked her, "Why didn't you ever come to get me? Didn't you wonder about me, what I was doing, what I had become, or if I was still alive?" With no answers provided, Antwone left his mother feeling like, "I saw her, but if I never see her again, I will be okay." Imagine being his mother and facing those types of questions from your child. My hurt goes out to all parents, myself included, because until we master how to be both human and a parent, we will always be close to the edge of a breakdown. Keeping the line of communication and forgiveness open can make some decisions less painful for all parties involved. **Romans 3:23 (NIV)** says, *"For all have sinned and fall short of the glory of God."* Being a parent does not exempt you from making wrong decisions or choices that affect those around you.

Before we close out this chapter, I want to leave you with a few tips on restoring your relationship with your children. As stated before, it will take work, but I promise you if done right, your relationship will end up being better than ever.

- **Apologize.**
  If you did something wrong, own it. There is nothing wrong with saying, "I'm sorry," "What can I do, if anything, to make right the wrong I did?" or even "It won't happen again." Then you will have to keep your word without expecting your child's feelings to change. The time it will take for their feelings to change is not in your control. The reality is those you have hurt will release their pain more slowly than you will want their forgiveness. Take responsibility for your actions; do not let your expectations keep you from doing what's right. **1 John 1:9 (NKJV)** — *"If we confess our sins, He is*

faithful and just to forgive us our sins and to cleanse us from all unrighteousness."

- **Expect nothing.**
  No one has to forgive you. More to the point, your children may forgive you and still not want you in their lives. Act without presumption that the relationship will improve. As the parent, you need to take the high ground. Reach out because you genuinely want to, whatever the result.

- **Speak your child's love language.**
  Gary Chapman's book *The Five Love Languages* explains a clear theory on how we express and receive love. You must speak your child's love language if you want a relationship to work. Some children's love language may be "quality time," and others may be "giving gifts." Both are great, and if they are not your love language, you have to understand and be willing to appreciate theirs, meet them where they are, and put their love language ahead of yours. You have to teach yourself to give love in the way your child wants to receive it.

- **Recognize that your child's perspective is valid.**
  There are at least two ways of seeing any situation.

My clients dealing with drug addictions always ask me, "Can't they see I'm trying?" My honest response is always, "Yes, your kids see your efforts, but that does not make their pain or experience any less real." Acknowledge this and let your children speak freely about how they are hurt. You may disagree, but your child has a right to his/her feelings. This is a humbling process where you might not like the words coming out of their mouths, but it's their pain and needs to be respected.

- **If you want the relationship, do the work.**
As their parent, your kids will always love you. However, both young and adult children will find other people to fill your role in your absence. Your child may be willing to meet you part of the way once you're back in their life, but the work is yours to do. If you want the relationship, you must humble yourself and do the work. Eventually, your child will respond positively if you consistently act in healthy, appropriate ways.

- **Do not give up.**
If the relationship means something to you, keep working on yourself and reaching out in healthy ways. Where there is breath, there is hope. If you are

doing the work, there is always a chance for something better. You may have hurt your child so bad that you don't think you deserve their forgiveness, but do not give up. Trust me, every child needs and wants their mother and father in their life.

Now, if you are a child who is trying to restore a relationship with your parent(s), here are some tips for you. When it comes to relationships, I am clear it is not always the parents who have to do the restoring but children, as well. Not having a healthy relationship with your parents can be a source of stress.

- **Work on your resentment first.**
  Instead of pushing negative emotions about your parents, have a close look at how they are. Examine all scenarios from the perspective of your parents. Was it intentional? Did they have only your interest at heart? At times, doing this can shift or reduce your feelings of resentment. If you want to talk to your parents, this will help you have a neutral conversation with less focus on placing blame. It will make the conversation more receptive rather than defensive.

- **Talk to them as friends.**

  Most children take the love and support of their parents for granted. Keep in mind that they also need and deserve appreciation and care. Treat them with respect just as you would treat your friend.

- **Slowly get back into the relationship.**

  Remember to take your time when trying to mend a broken relationship with your parents. The less pressure, the easier it will be for the both of you. It is better to take baby steps in the right direction than to take none. Move at a pace that is comfortable for you both.

- **Set new boundaries.**

  Setting good boundaries can be important in preventing unnecessary resentments and irritations— whether it involves establishing rules about calling before they visit, how often they can visit, or decisions regarding raising your children. You can set these boundaries firmly yet in a loving way.

Restore After Losing a Loved One

"Then Job sat on the ash-heap to show his sorrow. And while he was scraping his sores with a broken piece of pottery, his wife asked, 'Why do you still trust God? Why don't you curse him and die?'"

Job 2:8-9 (CEV)

Losing anyone is hard, but when faced with burying your parents, children, or spouse, it is a different kind of grief that, for most, never heals. It's been over twenty years since I lost my father, but it still feels like he passed yesterday. That is a pain that never goes away. Yes, it gets better but never totally removed. I also lost my best friend, college classmate, and godmother to my children, Steffanie Car. Since her passing, I have yet to find another person like her and often wonder why God called her home so soon. Even though I understand we all have a death date awaiting us, no one is ever prepared when it finally happens. So, for this chapter, I want to talk about how to restore after the death of a spouse.

Since I have not dealt with this personally, to help me convey this message, I talked to one of my close friends and fellow Howardites who experienced losing her spouse of nineteen years to brain cancer. My friend, Tara, was once happily married, raising her children, and traveling the world. She was living an exciting life full of fancy family vacations and happy holidays until she and her spouse received the news that her husband had life-threatening cancer. Now Tara is a young widow, mother of two beautiful children, a businessperson, and now living in her restoration of losing a spouse.

Before I share Tara's advice, let me say that I am truly grateful to her for allowing me the opportunity to share her story. This is a very personal and emotional story, and I applaud you, my friend, for being strong enough to relive this chapter in your life to be a blessing and help someone heal.

Tara and her husband were college sweethearts who met on Howard University's campus; they were both studying to become engineers. As fate would have it, they became fast friends and study partners, and not long after receiving their degrees, they married and had two beautiful children. As Tara told her story, she spoke of how she and her husband would always discuss their dreams and goals until late in the midnight hour. They got to achieve some of those dreams and goals. However, when he passed, she had to redirect her focus to being strong for their children while trying not to drown in her own grief. Often, she would cry out to God, questioning him on the decision to take her husband.

How many of you have questioned God about a decision that He knew was best? Despite knowing your spouse will not recover, how many of you allow them to suffer by keeping them hooked up to machines so that you can keep them here? Dealing with diseases and life-threatening situations is always hard because we do not want them to suffer, but at the same time, we do not want them to leave us. So how do we balance it all?

Having lost her husband, Tara is forced to live life without him but is blessed to have tons of happy memories that help her push on one day at a time. Tara offered one memory of how her husband would joke about her not being like Job's wife.

In the book of Job, Job faces many forms of suffering. He lost his children and wealth in a single day. He was then struck with painful sores over his entire body. His wife added to the pain by saying, "Are you still maintaining your integrity? Curse God and die!" **(Job 2:9–NIV)**. Instead of encouraging Job to endure faithfully, his wife said he should lie down and die. Even worse, she told him to curse God before he died. She saw God as the problem, the One who had abandoned Job in his time of trouble.

When Tara's husband was diagnosed with cancer, Tara never asked him to denounce God. Just like Job, Tara's husband suffered many losses. He was a sought-after engineer, but that career ended after he became blind. Once he lost the ability to eat solid food, Tara had to liquefy his food and feed him through a tube in his stomach. However, unlike Job's wife, Tara remained active in his caregiving and maintained her respect for God. She watched her soulmate deteriorate until God called him home.

The first and most important step of her restoration was learning to trust. "After his death, I felt numb and went through the motions because even though life was different, living and all that was required for surviving remained the same," she says.

Her daughter was a 10th grader when her husband passed. Her focus became making sure the children graduated from high school. After the second year of his passing, she started attending social events so she could interact with other adults and become a part of society in her new reality. She refers to her restoration as "Baby

Steps" because this is what it took for her to start being social again. Tara began by going out once a month and then twice a month. She knew it was important to be around people during her healing and restoration. She not only had to do this for herself, but she also had to do this for her family and her spouse's family, as well.

As the months and years went by, the restoration process got a bit easier for her. Part of the reason was she thought about how, if possible, her husband would have called her from heaven and given her a mouth full if she gave up on living. So, Tara realized she had to get herself together to continue what they had started. The restoration process for her was all about her children's happiness and reclaiming her life while never forgetting her husband. To this day, she wears a necklace around her neck with a beautiful pendant that holds a piece of her husband's hair inside.

The following are the "Baby Steps" that Tara took during her journey of restoration:

- Tara's first step to restoring was learning to trust. After losing someone you love, you may still believe in God and Jesus Christ. You may even hear the occasional whisper of the Holy Spirit. However, *trusting* God is a different story, especially if you feel numb, empty, brokenhearted, or angry. So, she had to learn to trust His will was best while believing her strength lived within Him.

- Her next step was never wavering as a mother. She shifted her grief and poured everything into the children, so even though they were grieving and missing their father, they still felt the love and support from their mother.

- The following step was realization and acceptance. Exactly one year after her spouse's death, she had a revelation based on an inside joke she shared with her husband before his passing. During his time of suffering, they thought he was Job, the one losing everything. Until one day, she realized she was, in fact, Job, the one losing someone who meant the absolute most to her.

- Her final step was to put herself back in the company of other adults. About two years after her husband's passing, she reentered society and started attending social events again. It was hard, but she pushed herself to stay a little longer each time instead of rushing back home to her safe place.

According to VeryWellMind.com, "Losing a spouse can be devastating, whether the death is sudden or following a prolonged illness. One day you are married; the next day you are single, alone, and grieving. Between the intense emotions, the lifestyle changes, and the many practical considerations that accompany the death of your spouse, you feel overwhelmed and anxious about your future. Over time, the grief will subside, and you will build a new life for yourself."

After speaking to my friend, I knew this article was spot-on. From the emotional roller coaster to the financial changes to trying to stay sane, death is not easy for anyone, but having a dedicated support system can make the grief and emptiness bearable.

In addition to Tara's baby steps to restoration, here are a few more you can consider:

- **You are not alone.**
  Although you may feel alone, there are other spouses dealing with the same loss. Be willing to reach out for grief counseling for yourself and your children. Romans 14:8 **(NIV)** says, *"If we live, we live for the Lord; and if we die, we die for the Lord."* So, whether we live or die, we belong to the Lord.

- **Be Patient.**
  Your restoration process will take some time, and that is okay. Once you take the first step, take another and then another. Pretty soon, you will be walking and then running. **Isaiah 41:10 (ESV)** says, *"Fear not, for I am with you; be not dismayed, for I am your God; I will strengthen you, I will help you, I will uphold you with my righteous right hand."*

- **Trust in the Lord; God knows your pain.**
  Proverbs 3:5-6 (ESV) says, *"Trust in the Lord with all your heart, and do not lean on your own understanding. In all your ways acknowledge him, and he will make straight your paths."* God knows what you're going through, and His promises are true. So, be encouraged. Your joy will come.

I am so proud of my friend because she made the decision not to give up and be in a continual state of hurt. Today, Tara has been blessed to see her children graduate from college. She is currently receiving grief counseling to properly do the work needed for further restoration, growth, and to accept her new reality. Now an empty nester, Tara is learning a new way of life in the beautiful home she and her husband built. She is happier now and even dating while looking for Mr. Right. She constantly gives God thanks for her restoration and the strength to keep marching forward. Like Tara and everyone else I've spoken to, myself included, they testified that restoration is a process that never really ends. Your life just gets better, and your belief grows stronger.

Preach, Preacha!

"Go, stand and speak to the people in the temple the whole message of this Life."

Acts 5:20 (NASB)

Although I have my ideas and experience about restoration, I felt it necessary to speak to Minister Cardinius Tyrone Byars of The Church of Yeshua Ha Mashiach in Lemon Grove, California, about the restoration process from a spiritual standpoint. I chose this minister to discuss this matter with because he is a person who had to kick an addiction of disobedience to be restored in the Word to serve.

When Minister Byars shared his personal story of his journey to becoming a clergy, I was truly inspired.

Charlotte Crumley-Arrington

Although Minister Byars believed in God and went to church every Sunday, he always showed up a little tipsy. He explained he could not wait until service was over so he could have another cocktail. One day, his friend, whom he always went to church with, heard a message from God telling him that they needed to stop showing up tipsy and hiding in the balcony during service. When his friend revealed this divine message from God, Minister Byars agreed to follow in his friend's footsteps, and within two years, they were completing their lessons in seminary school. From showing up to church tipsy to obtaining a master's degree in Divinity. Look at God!

Minister Cardinius Tyrone Byars has experienced the power of not only restoration but how God can use you through your bad acting and heathenism. They didn't know it, but God had bigger plans for both of them, and because they were obedient, God now gets all the glory. God needed to restore him for him to be used to be a blessing to others. Minister Byars also learned humility because although he knew he was wrong to show up in church that way, now he is able to have compassion for the next person who displays that same behavior.

I remember being at church and the pastor saying it does not matter how you come in the door, as long as you come in. This is a perfect example because God saved Minister Byars where he was, and now, he is humbly doing the same for others. He can bear witness that God will sit you down, turn you around, and place your feet on solid ground. One thing the minister stressed was that to be restored, one must be open to the process and believe it can and will happen.

As defined in the previous chapters, restoration is taking something and restoring it to its original state. It can also be the process of transforming something old and making it new. This same idea about restoration is also true as it relates to God's heart! Sin corrupts and weakens us. It even causes us to suffer loss and pain in many ways. Thus, God uses the power of restoration to bring his children back to Himself. Restoring oneself back into the Lord will lead to a life of peace and joy that we all want.

The Lord is about restoring people—physically, mentally, and spiritually. For example, the Word tells us that Adam and Eve were given a great garden of blessing, but they fell and were evicted from it. (**Genesis 3**). All hope was not lost, however, for God pledged to remedy their situation, as seen in Adam and Eve's hope for the Lord to provide a man who could lead the return to the garden (**v. 15; 4:1**). Centuries later, the nation of Israel repeated Adam's failure. Forgetting their covenant with God, the Israelites fell again and were evicted from the blessing of the divine presence in Canaan (**2 Kings 17:7–23**). Again, hope was not lost, for the righteous remnant hoped in the

Father to send a man who would lead the people back to blessing (**Luke 1:46–56; 2:22–38**). This man—the Lord Jesus Christ—did come, and even now, He is restoring His creation as God has promised.

Even though they all disobeyed or broke convent, God restored them to a place of moving forward. He did not stagnate anyone who disobeyed Him. He punished them, but they were able to fulfill the calling on their life. Regardless, if you are sick physically, struggling emotionally, or separated from God because of sin, He wants to restore that relationship with you. Restoring that relationship will once again refill your life with purpose and promise.

I know it's not a great feeling when we believe God has let us down or when He takes our loved ones from us or allows bad things to happen to us. Your faith and belief have been challenged, and you may grow weary of His grace. But let me tell you another secret—even though life has happened to you, He has never left your side. Nowhere in the Bible does it say God is going to leave you. In **John 14:27 (KJV)**, God said, *"Peace I leave with you, my peace I give unto you: not as the world giveth, give I unto you. Let not your heart be troubled, neither let it be afraid."* Also, in **Deuteronomy 31:6 (KJV)**, God assures us to, *"Be strong and of a good courage, fear not, nor be afraid of them: for the LORD thy God, he it is that doth go with thee; he will not fail thee, nor* *forsake thee."* Little do we know, God is our biggest advocate, cheerleader, and provider. A popular contemporary Christian song by Brian Johnson entitled "One Thing Remains" says it well with the lyrics, "His love never fails, and He never gives up on us." Another gospel song that speaks to my heart of restoration is "Break Every Chain," sung by Tasha Cobbs. We need God to break the chains that keep us in bondage with no hope for a better, brighter future.

As you can see, the power of restoration goes beyond the physical realm; it has a spiritual realm, as well. Restoring ourselves as humans is great, but reconnecting to the Father in the journey is mandatory. Throughout the restoration conversation, the Word of God was either provided by the person I interviewed or intertwined by the power of starting over and seeking God's help. When you invite God into your process, you allow Him to assist you in doing the work and make it better. Now, I need you to understand that God does NOT do your work; He assists you in the process. Some Christians suggest you pray and wait for God to deliver. I believe in the power of prayer and making your request known to the Lord, but God is no butler. He does not take your order and then deliver it on fine china. **James 2:14-20 (NKJV)** backs up my thought: *What does it profit, my brethren, if someone says he has faith but does not have works? Can faith save him? If a brother or sister is* *naked and destitute of daily food, and one of you says to them, "Depart in peace, be warmed and filled," but you do not give them the things which are needed for the body, what does it profit? Thus also faith by itself, if it does not have works, is dead. But someone will say, "You have faith, and I have works." Show me your faith without your works, and I will show you my faith by my works. You believe that there is one God. You do well. Even the demons believe—and tremble! But do you want to know, O foolish man, that faith without works is dead?"*

Faith without works is dead! Meaning you have to get up and execute. God can answer the prayer, but He will not live out the process for you. Whatever you commit to, He will be there to shower you with grace, blessings, and wisdom to reassure you that He is there with you. He is there for your transformation, not just to celebrate you at the goal line. He wants to prove to you that he is the Lord, your God, and His promise to you is yours if you so believe.

Minister Cardinius Tyrone Byars has expressed that sometimes you have to say more than one prayer to reassure God that what you are asking for is what you truly want. How many of you have prayed for something once and are still waiting? How many of you repeated your prayer in full detail of what you want, and the Lord placed you in the position to receive it? God is not going to answer just because you asked. When restoring your life and seeking God's assistance, your prayers must be clear and specific to what you need—not what you want or feel you deserve.

Now, God may delay your repeated prayers to ensure you are ready to handle them. For example, imagine seeking God for a good mate. You are very specific about what you desire this person to be, and then you happen to be in the right place at the right time to meet them. At first, they are everything you prayed for, but because you are not fully healed, you begin to mistreat the person, and they leave. Now you're back to praying for another mate while blaming them for why the relationship did not work. How do you think God will feel about Him rewarding you with your prayer only for you to lose it because you were not ready? This is why God delays your blessings longer than expected—to ensure you are ready and not just begging.

One of my favorite books is *The Secret*, and one of my favorite chapters is about the law of attraction. According to Mike Dooley, an author and international speaker, "Thoughts become things!" Through this most powerful law, your thoughts become the things in your life. Your thoughts become things! Say this over and over to yourself, and let it seep into your consciousness. Your thoughts become things! I challenge and encourage you to take three minutes out of your day every day to think about what your restoration looks and feels like. I promise you those thoughts will become a reality. I was so inspired that I started a challenge for people to manifest what they want in their life. My challenge is called "Manifestation Challenge 108". I encourage you to take the challenge and manifest what you want for yourself and your family.

As you see, to have restoration, there must be a standard that a person is being restored unto. In God's mind, that standard is not limited to a happy marriage, a positive net worth, or a specific job. God's standard for restoration is much higher. God's goal is to restore every person to His original intent for their life. That is why we are all targets of God's restoration. We are all in the process of restoration because God is restoring us to His original intent for humankind. I thank God that He is never content to leave us in a fallen state. Because Jesus died on the cross, God has a legal right to execute the deepest will of His heart, which is to restore on the earth. So, He has been at it ever since:

- He forgives our sins and restores us to eternal life when we receive His salvation in Christ Jesus.
- He heals our sicknesses and diseases, restoring our bodies to divine health.
- He restores our finances to a state of heavenly abundance when we tithe and give generously, even if we start at rock bottom.

- He redeems our minds from depression and fear, restoring us to a state of power, love, and a sound mind.
- He delivers us from sin and restores us to His original intent for us to walk before Him in holiness and purity.

Restoration is something every one of us needs in every area of life. We all need to be restored to God's original intent for us:

- to walk and talk with Him in person,
- to live seated with Christ Jesus in heavenly places,
- and to demonstrate His fullness and abundance on Earth.

Are you ready to be restored, seek God, accept prayer, receive healing, and be gracious to yourself? I promise you that if you follow the concepts mentioned in this book, the process will get easier, and you will reach your peace much faster.

Conclusion

As we approach this journey's end, let me first thank you for taking the Restoration 108 journey with me. Whatever the enemy has tried to take away from you, God wants to restore it. He wants to make it better than before. That is the kind of Father He is. Every day we have choices put before us. We can either engage in self-sabotaging behavior, complain while wallowing in the same awful conditions, or praise God and rise up.

One of the first things the enemy will try to steal from us is our joy. He wants us to be sorrowful and oppressed. Remember what it was like when you first were saved? There was an unspeakable joy. God does not want us to lose that joy. **Nehemiah 8:10** tells us, *"The joy of the LORD is your strength."* It is important for Christians to have joy in their life! But where does joy come from?

We tap into joy by hanging out with God! When we are in His presence, we have a new spring in our step and a new song in our heart. When spending time with Him, we take on His characteristics. We will have compassion for the person going through a divorce; we will give grace when someone makes a mistake or hurts our feelings; we will not judge someone who has been locked up in the penial system. We will take pity on the widowed, making sure her cup is full and her grief is acknowledged. Also, we will listen to the voice of God and be obedient to His word, accept responsibility for our mistakes, and be humble enough to ask for forgiveness.

Joel 2:25 (KJV) says, *"I will restore to you the years that the locust hath eaten, the cankerworm, and the caterpillar, and the palmerworm…"* Some of you have been down with many "worms" in your life. Some of you have lost years to an unhappy marriage. Some of you have lost years to health problems. But the Lord put something in my heart. He said, *"My mercy is greater than your mistakes, and I am a Master at fixing any disaster."* God loves us that much. Whether we have done things that are our fault, or whether it is the enemy who has stolen from us, God is still the restorer! God wants you to fulfill your dreams; He wants you to have joy; He wants you to have good health. Our God is an awesome God, and He has good things in store for us! Do not let the devil steal anything from you. I declare restoration over your life! Take what belongs to you, in the name of Jesus!

After reading this book, I hope and pray you now understand the power of restoration. Even though the processes provided may seem a bit overwhelming, let me reassure you that restoration is nothing more than being willing to humble yourself and ask God for healing. To some, restoration is similar to submission because it forces you to surrender your desire to God's will, allowing Him to lead. But the challenge is getting you to commit to a process that requires you to acknowledge, accept and take accountability for your choices. It removes you from blaming others and finding fault but causes you to stand in your truth and desire to transform towards better. Honestly, this process will provoke a lot of emotion while working to achieve the goal, but I promise you that through every tear and ounce of frustration, the reward is much greater.

As you embark on your restoration process, use this playbook as a reference when you get stuck or need support. You do not have to go on this journey blindly, nor are you alone. Although I am not physically present with you, the words within this book were written to serve you. I have poured everything I know, along with the contribution of others, to ensure we left no topic uncovered. I hope now that you have learned from man and heard from God, you feel safer in His arms and have faith that this process will return you to the peace and happiness you once had. I want you to be healed from all broken promises and bad decisions that hurt your spirit and impacted your soul. As a Certified Life Coach, my clients have begun seeking restoration after being introduced to it in church, and as someone who has lived it, I hope you now feel equipped.

As always, it has been my pleasure serving you on another journey, and if you need further help or are ready to start your process, please reach out to me on my social media platforms: Facebook@charlottecrumleyarrington and Instagram @charlottecrumleyarrington.

Before we close, let us leave in prayer:

Dear Lord,

We have seen the damage firsthand that storms can cause in our lives. We know within our hearts that this is not the end of the story, that You have something far greater to come.

Father, we ask today for Your hand in our lives. We pray for the restoration of our lives by Your process. That process may not look like what we would think or plan. But we know that because You see all that is, was, and is to come, You will ultimately do what is most compassionate and best. Father, today we come before Your holy throne to ask for Your restoration in our lives. We submit ourselves to Your ever-loving Will and kindness throughout. In Jesus' name, Amen.

Resources

How to Emotionally Heal Yourself? (Betterlyf.com)
https://www.betterlyf.com/articles/stress-and-anxiety/how-to-emotionally-heal-yourself/

5 Way to Give Yourself Grace by Rebecca Wertz (2020) (IridescentWomen.com)
https://iridescentwomen.com/2020/09/15/5-ways-to-give-yourself-grace/

Tom Lowenstein (2002) Collateral Damage: The Children of Prisoners (PrisonLegalNews.org)
https://www.prisonlegalnews.org/news/2002/jun/15/collateral-damage-the-children-of-prisoners/

Claire Gillespie (2020) What Is Generational Trauma? Here's How Experts Explain It (Health.com)
https://www.health.com/condition/ptsd/generational-trauma

Sheri Stritof (2020) Tips for Coping with the Death of a Spouse (VeryWellMind.com)
https://tinyurl.com/4t722wdn

The Secret by Rhonda Byrne
https://www.thesecret.tv/

About the Author

Charlotte Crumley Arrington is the mother of three phenomenal adult children, Joseph, Jessica, and Brian, and two amazing grandchildren, Kennedy and DeShawn. An in-demand motivational speaker, author, and life coach, Charlotte is enthusiastic about encouraging people to do what God has called them to do and teaching them the tangible skills to make it happen. Charlotte's diverse background and life experiences have prepared her for this fulfilling opportunity to motivate and coach with purpose. She has had the unique opportunity to travel worldwide, encouraging people to believe in the beauty of their dreams.

Charlotte was born in Honolulu, Hawaii, and raised in San Diego, California, by her amazing parents, Barbara and Jesse Crumley. She has an older brother, Duvall, and a sister, Latarsha. Charlotte comes from a family of believers. Her grandfather, Reverend Willis Brown, Sr., is the founder of Gethsemane Baptist Church in Charleston, South

Charlotte Crumley-Arrington

Carolina, which has been in Charlotte's family for over one hundred years and is now pastored by her first cousin, Reverend Herbert Harvey.

Charlotte is a proud graduate of Howard University in Washington, D.C., where she studied and received her BA in Speech Communications and U.S. History. During her time at Howard, Charlotte married recording artist Joe Tex, Jr. Having been blessed with strong communication and speaking skills, she has used her gift thousands of feet in the air amongst some of the world's most influential people. Charlotte always dreamed of becoming a flight attendant, and it was not long before her dream came true. She became a first-class flight attendant with American Airlines and continued with Swift Aviation, a private charter airline, as a lead flight attendant. While working with the private jet company, Charlotte served the White House Press Corps, NBA, NHL, MLB, MLS, A-list celebrities, presidents, and dignitaries of other countries.

Charlotte has a funny bone, which led her to serve as the opening act for several comedy shows starring Steve Harvey, Dave Chappelle, and Tommy Davidson. She has had the distinct honor of serving as the keynote speaker for an American Airlines flight attendant graduation and Health care giant LabCorp's company events also her Alma Mater, Howard University in Washington, D.C.

Currently, Charlotte works as a trainer for a biomedical

marketing firm in sunny California and is sold out on her mission, passion, and purpose of motivating people to reach their highest potential to follow their dreams, manifest their hearts' desires, and the power of expecting a miracle.

Other Books by
Charlotte Crumley Arrington

Greatness is not simply a fleeting thought. It has to be manifested. However, manifestation does not occur without ACTION, and action begins with YOU.

The first book in the dynamic *108* series, *The Message 108*, from debut author Charlotte Crumley Arrington, is the explosive playbook for readers who not only want to see their hearts' desires come true but also refuse to lose. In *The Message 108* (the divine number 108 signifying the time is now), Charlotte serves as your coach, providing you with creative strategies highlighting tangible skills that produce winning results. Everything you have been working, praying, and training for is set to become your reality. All you need are the right plays to make it happen. Every page, every encouraging word, and every strategy outlined in this book is designed to lead you to the success you are destined for and help you win the championship. Expect a miracle, follow your dreams, and watch as they come true. It is not just time to play—it's time to WIN!

Sometimes a kiss can speak a thousand words,
but it can also propel you to your destination!

Welcome aboard Flight 108, where becoming a flight
attendant is more than a dream. It is your destiny. Securing
a position in the highly competitive field can be a daunting,
exhausting, yet ultimately liberating process. In her
dynamic new book, *The Kissing Flight Attendant*, Author
Charlotte Crumley Arrington uses her electric personality,
quick wit, and endearing charm to meticulously help

aspiring attendants navigate each rigorous step that will take them from dreaming about being in the skies to taking flight.

Flight attendants have one of the most sought-after jobs in the world, but before they can soar the glamorous skies, they must conquer several strenuous interviews to snag the golden ticket and obtain their boarding pass. Finally, a book that not only teaches you all you need to know to secure the job but also entertains you along the way! Do you want to become a hero of the skies? Then sit back, buckle up, and let the amazing Kissing Flight Attendant escort you aboard Flight 108. Final destination? Success!

www.ingramcontent.com/pod-product-compliance
Lightning Source LLC
Chambersburg PA
CBHW060337130626
46553CB00003B/1034